To remove from book, detach carefully along perforation.
To play, please leave vinyl Soundsheet attached to backing card and place on turntable.

HOW TO READ THIS BOOK

The pages you are about to read come directly from a performance of my one-man show at the Brooks Atkinson Theatre in New York City. Picture yourself in the audience, in the first row center . . . unless you can't afford that kind of seat . . . so, the balcony. But wherever you are seated and ready to enjoy this book, it is important that you read this preface, because during the course of the book I'm going to ask you questions, just like I did to my live audiences. . . . And you better be prepared to give me answers because I have a way of checking up on you.

On the printed page I might sound somewhat arrogant. However, if you see me in person when I say these things you will realize that I say them without disdain, but with love and compassion. So, if you're not a schmuck you won't take it personally. If you are, it won't bother you either because you won't know the difference.

To tell you the truth, I not only call a person names but get applause as well, and even a standing ovation, which in all modesty I am getting on the stage every night.

When you finish this book, if you don't stand up and applaud you have either missed the humor in it or you don't appreciate it when a person gives you such big laughs for such a small price. Anyway, sit back in your seat, wherever you are . . . try to be normal, and enjoy yourself.

JACKIE MASON'S "THE WORLD ACCORDING TO ME!"

SIMON AND SCHUSTER

NEW YORK   LONDON   TORONTO   SYDNEY   TOKYO

"The World According to Me!" was produced in Los
Angeles and on Broadway at the Brooks Atkinson
Theatre by Nick Vanoff.

Published by Simon and Schuster
A Division of Simon & Schuster, Inc.
Simon & Schuster Building
Rockefeller Center
1230 Avenue of the Americas
New York, NY 10020

SIMON AND SCHUSTER and colophon are registered
trademarks of Simon & Schuster, Inc.

DESIGNED BY JOEL AVIROM

Manufactured in the United States of America

10 9 8 7 6 5 4 3 2 1

Library of Congress Cataloging-in-Publication Data
    Mason, Jackie.
The world according to me.

Based on the Broadway production with additional
original material.

1. American wit and humor. I. Title.
PN6162.M284 1987   818'.5402   87-17284
ISBN 0-671-64607-9

The author gratefully acknowledges permission to use the
following photographs: Bettmann Archive—6, 9, 10 (left), 10
(center), 15, 17 (top right), 18, 50, 62, 72 (top), 93, 96; Bizarro—
47; Dover—66, 67; © Deborah Feingold—2, 19, 25 (all photos), 38;
FPG International—26, 27, 59, 89; Ewing Galloway—17 (top left),
17 (bottom left), 17 (bottom right), 21, 23, 31, 32, 39, 48, 60–61,
63, 72 (bottom), 73, 75, 76, 79, 83, 86, 90; Image Bank—35, 65;
© Steven Lopez—45, 68; Rueters/Bettmann Newsphotos—40; ©
Martha Swope—8, 10 (right), 12 (all photos), 22, 29, 37, 46, 49,
58, 81, 92; © Michael Tighe—95; UPI/Bettmann Archive—33, 57;
UPI/Bettmann Newsphotos—14, 41, 42, 51, 52, 53, 54, 55, 64
(left), 64 (center), 64 (right); 69, 70

DEDICATION

Jyll Rosenfeld, my manager, for her love and devotion, who suf-
fered and struggled even more than I did for my own stardom

Morris Resner, my pal, for his endless energy in helping me with
this book

Morty Davis, with special gratefulness for his being a great friend
when I most needed it, and a fantastic human being

Nick Vanoff, my oldest and dearest friend, who has admired me so
long that I keep forgetting he's not Jewish, and without whom I
wouldn't have been on Broadway

"I see already
it's not for you."

MR. MASON'S AGENDA

THE BEGINNING

Hello, ladies and gentlemen.

For you to be reading this book you must be an intelligent person. This book is going to be hilarious from beginning to end. Many experts have said this is going to be the most sensational best-seller in this country. I only mention it in case you think it stinks, you'll know there's definitely something wrong with you, because intelligent people can't get over it.

I see already it's not for you.

This is a different kind of book than you ever saw before. It's got qualities you never heard of. It's the only book in the history of the world based on a show without furniture. Because when I was on Broadway I found out furniture had nothing to do with the show. When you come to see a show you want to hear what people got to say. Who wants to see "Here's a table, here's a chair." Furniture's coming and going. The sofa's coming. The chairs are leaving. Whose business is it? What's that got to do with the show? When you go to a furniture

"Who is he to do a show all by himself?"

9

store do they show you a comedian?

In your case, the only furniture you need for reading is a chair—or a couch—or a bed. If you like to stand—it's up to you.

Another quality that this book has that you don't see too often is that it's based on a one-man show, which disturbs a lot of people. They say, "Who is he to do a show all by himself?" It hurts them to see a Jew make such a comfortable living. It's killing them. First of all, you don't need two people for a show any more than you need furniture. People think the more people they see the better the show. By the time they see ten people—"What a show!" Fifty people—"Is this a show!"

"Was it any good?"

"I don't know, but was it *busy!*"

This more-than-one business is stupid, because all the great things that were ever accomplished in this country were accomplished by one person working alone. You don't need two people. Soon as you see two people, nothing comes of it. One person does every great thing throughout history. Take a look. Albert Einstein, was he a great man?

Pay attention!

One of the greatest people who ever lived was Albert Einstein. That's right. Created the whole theory of relativity all by himself. Now there were thousands of people with nothing to do. He didn't say, "Mister, help

Solo Acts

EINSTEIN   MICHELANGELO   MASON

out, I got a problem here." Never said a word. He did it alone.

Michelangelo, was he a great man? (If you can't answer this question, you'll never understand this book.) As great as Michelangelo was, he did it alone. He worked the whole Sistine Chapel, painted it all by himself. Now there were thousands of people walking around with brushes. Do you think he said to them, "Mister, help out?" Never. He did it alone.

Alone . . . it took him thirty years because the man was a schmuck. Because the truth is it doesn't have to take thirty years to paint the ceiling. I got a brother-in-law, two kitchens and a toilet, an hour and a half . . . because he didn't use a brush. A roller does the same thing! Do you understand this?

Here's another example. You're lucky I'm not busy. I'll explain everything to you. How many people do you marry?

Pay attention! This is important!

If you're a normal person you only marry one human being. Now, if more is better how come you don't marry two or four or six or twelve? The more people you need, the sicker you are. That's what any psychologist will tell you. Now, there are thousands of brilliant people. How come you only need one?

Wake up!

The first sign of mental instability is that you need more than one person. What do you think psychologists refer to when they talk about the idea of commitment? What do they mean by commitment?

So?

By commitment, they mean the ability to relate to one other human being, because that's all you need. That's what they mean

. . . Looking and waiting and looking . . .

when they talk about a one-on-one relationship. That's a sign of normality.

You're sick if you need a lot of people. That's right. A normal person only needs one person, because through that one person you can relate to every emotion, every need, every feeling, every thought, every point of view, every significance of everything you have on your mind, on every level, with just one person. That's all you need. Because if you've found that one person you can thank God that you found him.

You should thank God, because now you can spend the rest of your life with that one person sitting in the house . . . looking and looking . . . looking and waiting and looking . . . and that's it. He's gone to the toilet. He came back from the toilet. He's not sure . . . he might go . . . he's almost going. . . . He's watching television. He's almost watching. He forgot to watch. He wants to watch. He's changing the station. He changed it already. He don't need it. He has it. He wants something. He don't want it. He wants it. He'll take it. He has it. . . . And *you* say thank God you found a schmuck like this! This is what you got to look forward to, mister?

Compared to that, this book is a hit!

"The truth is, you don't *need* sex..."

SEX

most people when they go to see shows are only interested in some kind of sexual story—sex, sex, sex. Every show and every book today is about nothing but sex. Mine is the only clean production left. Every major novel is about sex. Every book, every story, every picture. That's all you ever hear about is sex.

There was a time when sex couldn't be mentioned at all. It was considered vulgar and filthy. Now you can't find any form of entertainment that isn't just the opposite. Nothing but sex. The theme or the underlying thought, the philosophy, the basic idea behind every premise is about nothing but sex. Why is that?

Wake up and pay attention to what I'm telling you!

The truth is you don't need sex for the theme of every show. There are more important things than sex. Why don't they talk about music? Did you ever think of that? Don't you think music is more important than sex? I mean, for a person in your condition?

I always thought that music was more important. I always did. Then I started to notice that if I don't hear a concert for a year and a half, it don't bother me.

Tell me, is it hurting you to laugh so much? I know this is probably breaking a lifetime habit for you . . . but frankly, I don't care if you laugh or not. I got enough money to last me the rest of my life . . . unless I want to buy something. I'll be honest with you. The kind of spender I am, I'll never notice if I make a living or not anyway.

Who needs a lot of money? A sick person needs a lot of money. Always trying to make impressions that serve no purpose. They're spending money for nothing. Like an average guy makes a date with a girl. It costs him one hundred dollars, two hundred dollars. I make a date with a girl, it costs me nothing. Nothing! I come up to her house. She wants to go out. I let her go! What's my business? I have to follow her around?

Let's be honest, why does a guy take a girl out in the first place? He takes her out so he can be with her when she comes back. I'm there already. Where am I going?

Do you know what's also very interesting? There's a great study

"Mister, tell me, is it hurting you to laugh so much?"

She was raised
to think that
she shouldn't do it.

you can make about the sheer hypocrisy of the whole dating system in this country. The most honest man at this time becomes a total fraud. A guy takes out a girl. For what reason? He takes out a girl. For what reason? He takes her out because she appeals to him sexually. Let's be honest about it. It's not nice to mention it, but that's what it is. If it wasn't sex, he'd take out his brother-in-law.

You're not supposed to mention sex because she was raised to think that she shouldn't do it. You were raised to think that you should! But if you mention it, you would lose her because you have to prove that you don't want it in order to get it. The whole trick is to figure out how to get it without talking so she can do it without hearing! You can't admit that it's sex, because it's not nice, so social courtesy requires that you say something about a dinner.

Everybody who ever was attracted to a girl says, "Did you eat yet?"

What does a dinner got to do with what you want from that girl? Does a dinner have something to do with it?

Mister?

Who the hell cares if she ate or not? What you want from her, you're gonna get it in a restaurant? Everybody says, "Did you eat yet?" Are you a caterer? Do you care?

They're all phonies and they all have to talk about something that has nothing to do with a date. I don't mention dinners because I'm the only honest person left. I stand outside of a restaurant. I wait to see who ate already. On her way out I say, "Hello, you ate? Good." Otherwise, next!

Do you understand this?

Let me tell you something important because there might be a lot of hookers reading this book. What makes a person a hooker? Let's take your case. . . . Please don't be offended if you really are a hooker. But if you are, I hope you're Jewish, because if I call an Italian girl a hooker I could get killed altogether. That's right, that's right. You call an Italian girl a hooker, you better be very careful or somebody'll kill you. You

Did you eat yet?

"Funny, you don't look like a hooker."

call a Jewish girl a hooker—she's thrilled! "No kidding, I look like a hooker? How come I never heard that before? When did you notice it?" And they start carrying on and looking in the mirror. . . .

The truth is that the Jewish girls are right. The truth is that it's a great compliment. It is a great compliment to say that someone looks like a hooker because, in effect, what you're saying is that she looks like a beautiful woman. You have to be a beautiful woman to make a living in that field. A short fat yenta with a mustache . . . what are you going to give her, eighty cents?

To say that someone looks like a wife is no compliment. Because a wife could look bitter, pathetic, morose, ridiculous and nauseating . . . and it's going to cost you fifty thousand dollars a year if you're Jewish. That's right. Even if you're Italian . . . all right, twelve thousand. Let's say you're a Puerto Rican . . . a dollar and a quarter. . . .

I'll bet you're having a great laugh now! But I told you, I don't care if you laugh or not. I hope you don't think I'm saying that because I'm an arrogant person. I'm not and I hate an arrogant person. I can tolerate anything—even people like you reading my book!

All great
men were
rejected.

PSYCHIATRY

When I tell you I don't care if a person laughs or not it's because I know who I am. That's not arrogance. That's mental health.

Any psychologist will tell you that if you know who you are it doesn't matter what other people think of you. The measure of yourself should be within yourself. You should have enough confidence to know who you are and not care what other people think. Because all great men were always rejected, neglected, and even hated in their own lifetime.

I'm talking to you, personally.

All great men were rejected.

You'll never have this problem.

Study history—you're not that busy. You'll find every great man was hated in his own lifetime. What is the reason for that? Because nobody is going to admit that he's stupid or simple or that he doesn't know what you're talking about. So he'll convince himself that *you're* nuts! That's why all great men are considered nuts in their lifetime, because other people don't know what the hell they're talking about. That's why it doesn't bother me that you might think I'm nuts, because I know who I am. That's right. This is a great trick in life, to know who you are.

There was a time I didn't know who I was. Thank God, now I know. I don't know if you heard about it. I went to a psychiatrist. I'm not ashamed to admit it. It's because I didn't know who I was. He took one look at me and said right away, "This is not you."

I said, "If this is not me, then who is it?"

He said, "I don't know either."

I said, "Then what do I need you for?"

He said, "To find out who you are."

I said to myself, "If I don't know who I am, how do I know who to look for? And even if I find me, how do I know it's me? Besides, if I want to look for me, why do I need him? I can look myself. Or I could take my friends. We'd know where I was. Besides, what if I find the real me and I find out he's even worse than me? Why do I need him? I don't make enough for myself . . . I need a partner? Ten years ago I'd be glad to look for anybody. Now I'm doing good. Why should I look for him? He needs help? Why doesn't he look for me?"

He said, "The search for the real you will have to continue. That'll be a hundred dollars, please."

I said to myself, "If this is not the real me, why should I give *him* a hundred dollars? *I'll* look for the real me. Let *him* give him a hundred dollars. . . . But what if I find the real me and he doesn't think it's worth a hundred dollars? Then I've

"If this is not me, then who is it?"

stuck my money with the real him."

Then I said, "For all I know the real me might be going to another psychiatrist altogether. Might even be a psychiatrist himself. Wouldn't it be funny if you're the real me and you owe *me* a hundred dollars?"

I said, "I'll tell you what. I'll charge you fifty dollars and we'll call it even."

You
only see
people in
restaurants.

BEVERLY HILLS

I hope you don't get the wrong impression. I'm thrilled about getting to Broadway and thrilled that you still have this book in your hands. It doesn't take that much to make me happy.

I was even happy in Beverly Hills because I was a big hit there, but in Beverly Hills it's no trick. Everybody's a sensation there. Anybody who lives in Beverly Hills can't get over themselves. They can't get over themselves. They walk around, "Oh yeah, I live in Beverly Hills."

"You too?"

"Oh yeah."

They don't walk, they dance! They feel like a celebrity just by living there. Why anybody would want to live there I don't know.

You never see a person in Beverly Hills. Never a person! Just trees and shrubbery. Never see a person. See gates opening and closing. You don't know why. There are ninety thousand homes, but no people. It looks like everybody passed away a hundred years ago and left the houses there. You could ride around for a year and a half, and never see a person. There's a gate, there's a Japanese gardener. He's

27

coming. He's going. Japanese gardeners are walking around, they don't know why, they don't know where. Nobody ever hired them. Nobody ever paid them. . . .

You never see a person on the streets, you only see people in restaurants. They're all talking deals. In the millions. They're all sitting in restaurants and they're talking deals. In Beverly Hills no deal is less than ninety million—and this is *without* a job. They don't need a job. All over America a deal is three hundred dollars, four hundred and fifty. In Beverly Hills, ninety million . . . a zillion! Then the check comes for a dollar twenty-five and people run like sonsofbitches. . . .

In Beverly Hills everyone is unemployed, but they're all producers. In New York if you're unemployed you go to an unemployment office, but over there everybody's a producer. Nobody has a job but they all have a card.

"I'm a producer. Here's my card."

That's all they produce—cards. And they don't have just one card. They have thousands of cards in every pocket.

"Here's the company I'm buying . . . I'm selling . . . This is the one I went into. This is the one I'm coming out of. Is this a company!"

Cards and cards . . .

"Are you making a living?"

"Not right now, but . . ."

He's starving to death, but the printer is making a fortune!

Do you know what else they all have? They all have a Mercedes. A Mercedes is like a uniform. If you're ever in Beverly Hills you'll know that you can't call yourself a producer without a Mercedes. They all have a card and a Mercedes. Without a Mercedes you look like a bum.

In every other part of this country you have a Cadillac you look like a hero. You look like a celebrity. People can't get over how successful you are if you can afford a Cadillac! But in Beverly Hills if a guy has a Cadillac, he's embarrassed by it. He has a whole speech prepared: "This is not my regular car. I don't know who left it here. I told my sister-in-law, 'Get your car out of here!' "

I pity a gentile in Beverly Hills, because if a gentile can't afford a Mercedes he has no excuse. What can he tell you? He has to *admit* he can't afford it. If a Jew can't afford a Mercedes, he thanks God he's Jewish. Every Jew who can't afford a Mercedes has the same speech: "You think I'm going to buy a *German* car?"

Meanwhile everything in his house is from Germany. Everything!

"You think I'm going to buy a German car?"

His camera's from Germany . . . his watch is from Germany . . . his shoes . . . Everything is from Germany up to eighty-seven dollars and fifty cents. As soon as he found out a car was fifty thousand dollars, "Those Nazi bastards!"

You know what's even funnier? (Not to you. I'm talking about a normal person.) What's even funnier is how people who have a Mercedes are always embarrassed and sick whenever they see a Rolls-Royce. There's more Rolls-Royces in Beverly Hills than anywhere else in the world. So just when a person feels like he's a hit because he owns a Mercedes then there comes one Rolls-Royce after another. Now he's embarrassed all over again because the same need to impress people that made him buy a Mercedes is the same reason why he would rather have a Rolls-Royce. The only reason he doesn't have a Rolls-Royce is because either he can't afford it or is too cheap to buy it. So now he needs a speech, too: "I wouldn't take it if you gave it to me for nothing! Who wants a Rolls-Royce? It's a waste! The worst! They're always in the shop. You can't get them out of the shop!"

I said, "So how come I see so many Rolls-Royces around here?"

"They're all on their way to the shop!"

"So how come I see so many Rolls-Royces around here?"